Learn Ember.js

A. De Quattro

Copyright © 2024

Guide to Ember.js

1. Introduction to Ember.js

Ember.js is an open-source JavaScript framework used for creating complex and interactive web applications. Created in 2011 by Yehuda Katz, Tom Dale, and other developers, Ember.js has emerged as one of the leading client-side frameworks used for developing single page applications (SPAs) and web applications that require high interactivity.

Ember.js provides a solid and organized structure for developing complex web applications, allowing developer teams to work efficiently and collaboratively. With its convention-based approach and numerous built-in features, Ember.js simplifies the development process and enables the creation of robust and scalable applications.

1.1 What is Ember.js

Ember.js is a front-end JavaScript framework based on the Model-View-ViewModel (MVVM) architectural pattern. The framework provides a set of tools and libraries for creating complex and interactive user interfaces, managing presentation logic and application data separately.

Ember.js is based on a set of conventions and best practices that facilitate application development and promote code maintainability. The framework includes numerous modules and components that simplify application state management, event handling, and DOM manipulation.

Some key features of Ember.js include:

- Routing: The framework includes a powerful and flexible routing system that allows efficient management of the various screens of the application. Ember.js routing is based on hierarchical URLs that correspond to different application resources.

- Templating: Ember.js uses the Handlebars templating language for creating dynamic and reactive views. Handlebars allows for the insertion of dynamic data within HTML markup, facilitating the creation of complex user interfaces.

- Data binding: Ember.js supports two-way binding of data between application models and views. This mechanism helps keep application data and views synchronized, making application state management easier.

- Components: Ember.js includes a component system that allows for the creation of reusable and modular UI elements. Components can be encapsulated and composed to create complex and flexible interfaces.

1.2 Benefits of Using Ember.js

Using Ember.js for web application development offers numerous benefits for both developers and end users. Here are some of the key advantages of using Ember.js:

- Productivity: Ember.js provides an organized and convention-based structure that simplifies application development. With its clear architecture and numerous integrated features, Ember.js enables efficient and collaborative coding.

- Scalability: Ember.js is designed for creating scalable and complex web applications. The framework offers tools for application state management and code structuring, making it easy to handle large applications.

- Performance: Ember.js is optimized to ensure high performance of web applications. The framework includes efficient caching and rendering mechanisms that help reduce loading times and improve user experience.

- Community: Ember.js has a large community of active developers who contribute to the framework's development and improvement. The community offers support, resources, and additional plugins that enhance Ember.js functionality.

- Documentation: Ember.js has detailed and up-to-date documentation that provides information on all framework features and best practices. The documentation includes code examples, guides, and tutorials to facilitate learning and usage of Ember.js.

1.3 Installation and Initial Configuration

To start using Ember.js, you need to follow some steps for installing and configuring the framework. Here is a step-by-step guide to install Ember.js and create a basic project:

1. Install Node.js and npm: Ember.js uses Node.js and npm as package managers. Before installing Ember.js, make sure you have installed Node.js on your system. You can download Node.js from the official website and follow the installation instructions.

2. Install Ember CLI: Ember.js provides a command-line tool called Ember CLI that facilitates project creation and management. To install Ember CLI, run the following command using npm:

```
npm install -g ember-cli
```

3. Create a new Ember.js project: Once Ember CLI is installed, you can create a new Ember.js project by running the following command:

```
ember new your_project_name
```

This command creates a new folder with the project name and initializes a new Ember.js project within it.

4. Start the application: After creating the project, you can start the Ember.js application by running the following command:

```
cd your_project_name
```

ember serve
```

This command starts a local server and launches the Ember.js application at http://localhost:4200.

5. View the application: Open your browser and visit http://localhost:4200 to view the basic Ember.js application. You will see the Ember.js welcome screen and can start exploring the framework's features and structures.

Ember.js is a powerful and flexible front-end framework that simplifies the development of complex and interactive web applications. Thanks to its organized structure and convention-based approach, Ember.js allows developer teams to work efficiently and collaboratively, creating robust and scalable applications.

With its numerous built-in features and large community of active developers, Ember.js is a popular choice for developing high-quality single page applications and web applications. If you are looking for a versatile and high-performing front-end framework, Ember.js
```

could be the ideal solution for your next web development project.

2. Fundamentals MVC (Model-View-Controller) Router Template Components Ember.js Services

Installation:

To install Ember.js on your computer, you need to follow a few steps:

1. Create a new folder on your computer where you want to install Ember.js.

2. Open the terminal and navigate to the created folder using the command `cd folder_path`.

3. Once in the folder, you can install Ember.js using the npm (Node Package Manager) package manager by running the command `npm install -g ember-cli`.

4. After the installation is complete, you can create a new Ember.js project by running the command `ember new project_name`.

5. After creating the project, you can start it for the first time by running the command `cd project_name` followed by the command `ember serve`.

6. Now you can open your browser and type `http://localhost:4200/` to view the newly created Ember.js application.

7. During the development of your Ember.js application, you can use the `ember generate` command to create new components, models, controllers, or routes.

8. Once your application development is complete, you can build and distribute it by running the `ember build` command, which will compile the application and create a `dist` folder containing the static files ready to be deployed to a web server.

By following these steps, you will be able to install and start developing web applications with Ember.js on your computer.

2.1 MVC (Model-View-Controller)

MVC, which stands for Model-View-Controller, is a widely used architectural pattern in software development that separates the components of an application into three different parts to improve code management, maintainability, and scalability.

The Model represents the application's data and defines the business rules, handling data access, modification, and validation. It is responsible for interacting with the database or other external data sources.

The View is responsible for presenting data to users, displaying the user interface and interacting with them. It is separated from the Model and deals with displaying and updating data in a way that is consistent with the underlying Model.

The Controller acts as an intermediary between the Model and the View, handling user interactions and coordinating the flow of data between them. It is responsible for business logic and processing user requests, sending commands to the Model to fetch or modify data and updating the View accordingly.

By separating responsibilities between Model, View, and Controller, it becomes easier to modify and test the different components of the application individually, increasing code maintainability and flexibility.

2.2 Router

The Router is a fundamental component of an Ember.js application that manages user navigation between different pages of the application. It defines routes, or paths, that users can take within the application and associates each route with specific controllers and templates.

Ember.js Router uses a URL-based approach to handle user navigation, creating an intuitive and familiar interface for users. Each route is associated with a unique URL that represents the user's current location within the application and allows them to easily navigate back to a particular page or resource.

Ember.js Router also offers advanced features for handling dynamic routes and URL parameters, allowing developers to create flexible and customizable applications.

Thanks to the Router, it is possible to create a smooth and consistent navigation experience for users, improving the usability and accessibility of the application.

2.3 Template

The Template is a component of Ember.js that defines the layout and structure of the application's user interface. By using the Handlebars templating language, you can easily create reusable and dynamic components that interact with the Model and Controller of the application.

Ember.js Templates allow you to separate data presentation from business logic, improving code maintainability and flexibility. Each Template is associated with a specific route of the application through the Router, allowing developers to create custom and responsive interfaces for different pages and sections of the application.

Developers can use Handlebars directives within Templates to dynamically insert data, properties, and presentation logic, making the user interface flexible and interactive. Additionally, Ember.js Templates support composition and inheritance, making it easy to create atomic and composite components that can be easily reused in different contexts.

Thanks to Ember.js Templates, it is possible to create feature-rich and customizable user interfaces without having to write large amounts of HTML and CSS code, simplifying development and enhancing user experience.

2.4 Components

Components are one of the main features of Ember.js that allow for the creation of modular and reusable user interfaces. A component is an isolated portion of logic and layout that can be embedded within a Template to create complex and dynamic interfaces.

Ember.js Components can be easily created using the Ember CLI component generator and can be composed or nested within other Components or Templates to create complex and customized interfaces. Each Ember.js component consists of a JavaScript file, a Handlebars template file, and a CSS stylesheet file, allowing for efficient organization of presentation logic and user interaction.

Ember.js Components are standalone and isolated, allowing for the separation of application functionalities into distinct and cohesive units that can be easily reused and tested. Additionally, Components support custom properties and events, enabling the creation of dynamic and interactive interfaces that respond to user actions.

Thanks to Ember.js Components, it is possible to create modular and flexible user interfaces that can be easily extended, customized, and reused in different application contexts, improving code maintainability and scalability.

2.5 Ember.js Services

Ember.js Services are shared and reusable objects that provide functionality and data across different parts of the application. Ember.js Services are instantiated only once during the application's lifecycle and can be injected into Controllers, Components, Routes, and other Services to share common data and functionality.

Ember.js Services allow for the separation of business logic and data management from presentation and user interface, improving code modularity and maintainability. Thanks to Services, it is easy to create shared functionalities that can be easily updated and tested without repeating code in multiple parts of the application.

Ember.js Services support Dependency Injection, which automatically injects Services into Controllers, Components, and other parts of the application, simplifying dependency management and ensuring data and business logic consistency throughout the application.

Additionally, Ember.js Services can be easily extended with additional modules and custom functionalities, allowing for specialized services that adapt to the specific needs of the application.

Thanks to Ember.js Services, it is possible to create robust and scalable applications that maintain data and functionality consistency throughout the application, improving the experience for developers and users.

3. Ember.js Template Components

The basic building block of Ember.js is based on components, which represent reusable and modular parts of the user interface. Each component has its own internal state, which can be modified through actions and properties. Components can be composed together to create complex hierarchies of user interfaces.

Route
Routes in Ember.js are responsible for handling the data needed to display a specific section of the application. Routes can fetch data from the backend or other services and make it available to the component templates. Routes can also manage the transition between different pages of the application.

Model
The model in Ember.js represents the data of a certain type of resource, such as a user or an instance of an object. Models can be defined using Ember Data, a framework for data management in Ember.js. Models can have relationships with each other, which can be defined using Ember Data and used to fetch

related data.

Controller
Controllers in Ember.js are responsible for managing the state and display logic of a specific section of the application. Controllers can modify the state of models and respond to events generated by components and routes. Controllers can also expose data to the views, making them available for display.

Service
Services in Ember.js are singleton objects that can be used to share data and functionality between different components, routes, and controllers. Services are injected into the Ember.js application and can be used to manage cross-cutting concerns, such as event handling or communication with external services.

Bindings
Bindings in Ember.js are a mechanism that allows dynamically linking two properties of different objects, so that when one of them changes value, the other is automatically updated as well. Bindings are used to keep the state of different components in sync and to update the display in real-time.

Computed Properties

Computed properties in Ember.js are dynamically calculated properties, whose value depends on other properties or data present in the application. Computed properties are defined within a controller or component and are automatically updated when the dependencies change value. Computed properties are used to efficiently and reactively calculate derived values.

Observers

Observers in Ember.js are functions that are executed reactively when a specific property or data changes value. Observers are used to monitor the state of a specific part of the application and perform actions or updates in response to changes. Observers allow for reactive event handling and keeping different elements of the application in sync.

Routing
Routing in Ember.js handles navigation within the application, defining routes that correspond to specific URLs. Routes are mapped to corresponding controllers and templates, allowing different sections of the application to be displayed based on the requested URL. Routing in Ember.js utilizes the concept of nested routes to represent complex hierarchies of navigation.

Ember Data
Ember Data is a framework integrated into Ember.js for managing data within the application. Ember Data provides a unified interface for retrieving, modifying, and saving data from various sources, such as a RESTful backend or a local database. Ember Data uses models and relationships defined to efficiently manage data within the application.

Ember Octane
Ember Octane is a new version of Ember.js introduced to provide greater clarity and ease of development. Ember Octane eliminates outdated concepts, reduces code verbosity, and promotes the use of the framework's most modern features. Ember Octane includes Glimmer components, RFC-based routing,

decorators, and other enhancements for a better development experience.

Testing
Ember.js provides a set of tools for running automated tests on your code to ensure that the application functions correctly and that changes do not introduce regressions. Ember.js supports unit tests, integration tests, and acceptance tests, and provides an integrated testing framework that facilitates writing, executing, and debugging tests.

Addons
Addons in Ember.js are feature packages that can be added to the application to extend its capabilities. Addons can provide components, services, helpers, templates, and any other functionality that can be encapsulated and reused across different Ember.js applications. Addons can be installed via npm and configured within the application.

Ember.js is an open-source framework for building interactive web applications, based on the Model-View-ViewModel (MVVM) architectural pattern. One of the fundamental concepts of Ember.js is that of components, which are reusable and self-contained code blocks that represent parts of the user interface. Ember.js components consist of a template, defining the component's HTML structure, and a JavaScript file that handles the component's behavior and logic.

An example of a component in Ember.js could be a navigation menu, containing a list of links to different sections of the site. The template of the component could be similar to this:

```
<nav>
  <ul>
    {{#each links as |link|}}
      <li>{{#link-to link.route}}{{link.text}}{{/link-to}}</li>
    {{/each}}
  </ul>
</nav>
```

In this template, the `{{#each}}` block is used to iterate over an array of `links` objects and generate an `<li>` element for each link. The `{{#link-to}}` block is used to generate a link that redirects to a specific route in the application.

The JavaScript file of the component may contain the definition of the `links` array and the logic to handle any events or actions associated with the component:

```
import Component from '@ember/component';

export default Component.extend({
  links: [
    { route: 'home', text: 'Home' },
    { route: 'about', text: 'About' },
    { route: 'contact', text: 'Contact' }
  ]
});
```

In this example, the `links` array contains objects representing the navigation menu links, with the route path and display text for each link.

Route and Model
Another key concept in Ember.js is routes and models, which are responsible for retrieving the data to display in the application and handling navigation between different pages. Routes in Ember.js correspond to a specific

URL of the application and are associated with a model, which represents the data to display. When the user navigates between the different routes of the application, Ember.js loads the data related to the current route model and renders the corresponding view.

In this example, the "posts" route defines a `model()` method that returns all `post` objects from the application's store. The store is a service provided by Ember.js that manages data caching and communication with the backend. When the user accesses the "posts" route, Ember.js loads the data from the model and passes it to the corresponding template for display.

Template with examples

The template associated with the "posts" route might look like this:

In this template, the `{{#each}}` block is used to iterate over all `post` objects returned from the model and generate an `<li>` element for each article, displaying its title.

Controller and Actions
Another important concept in Ember.js is controllers and actions. Controllers are

responsible for managing the state and logic of the application, while actions allow you to handle user events such as button clicks or keyboard inputs. Ember.js controllers are associated with a specific route and contain the properties and methods necessary to handle user interaction with the application. Un esempio di controller e azioni in Ember.js potrebbe essere un controller associato alla route "posts" che gestisce la logica per aggiungere un nuovo articolo. La definizione del controller potrebbe essere simile a questa:

```
import Controller from '@ember/controller';

export default Controller.extend({
  actions: {
    addPost(title, content) {
      let newPost = this.store.createRecord('post', {
        title: title,
        content: content
      });
      newPost.save();
    }
  }
});
```

In this example, the controller defines a method `addPost()` that creates a new `post` object with the title and content passed as arguments and saves it to the backend using the `save()` method. This action can be triggered by a form in the corresponding template.

Service and Dependency Injection
Another important concept in Ember.js is that of services and dependency injection. Services are shared objects that maintain the state and logic of the application, and can be accessed from different parts of the application. For example, a service could be used to handle user authentication or make HTTP calls to the backend.

To use a service in Ember.js, you need to inject it into routes, controllers, or components where it is needed. This ensures that the service instance is unique and shared among all components that use it.

An example of a service in Ember.js could be a service for managing user authentication. The definition of the service could be similar to this:

```
import Service from '@ember/service';

export default Service.extend({
  isAuthenticated: false,

  login(username, password) {
    // Make a call to the backend to verify credentials
    // Set isAuthenticated to true if authentication is successful
  },

  logout() {
    // Make a call to the backend to logout
    // Set isAuthenticated to false
  }
});
```

In this example, the service defines two methods, `login()` and `logout()`, which respectively handle user login and logout. This service can be injected into routes, controllers, or components where it is necessary to check the user's authentication status.

Ember.js is a comprehensive and powerful framework for developing modern web applications, offering advanced architectural tools and patterns for creating dynamic and responsive user interfaces. The fundamental concepts of Ember.js, such as components, routes, controllers, services, and actions, allow for efficient organization and management of the application code, creating a smooth and intuitive user experience.

Using Ember.js requires a learning curve, but once familiarity with its concepts and APIs is acquired, it is possible to quickly and efficiently develop complex and scalable web applications. Ember.js also offers a wide range of plugins and addons that extend the framework's capabilities and customize the development experience.

In conclusion, Ember.js is an ideal choice for the development of large web projects that require a solid and scalable structure, with a focus on productivity and ease of maintenance. With its solid fundamental concepts and powerful features, Ember.js remains one of the most comprehensive and powerful frontend frameworks currently available on the market.

4. Route Model Controller in Ember.js

Route, Model, Controller are three fundamental concepts in Ember.js, a JavaScript framework based on the MVC (Model-View-Controller) paradigm that facilitates the development of complex and dynamic web applications. In this context, Route handles application navigation, Model represents the underlying data, and Controller manages user interface logic. Let's see in detail how Route, Model, Controller work in Ember.js.

1. Route:
The Route in Ember.js is responsible for managing application navigation. Each route corresponds to a defined path in the application's URL and determines which data model should be loaded and which template (the view) should be displayed. Routes in Ember.js are defined within the "app/routes" directory and extend from the Ember.Route class.

For example, if we have an application that manages a list of users, we could have a route called "users" that handles displaying all users. The definition of this route could look like this:

```javascript
// app/routes/users.js
import Route from '@ember/routing/route';

export default class UsersRoute extends Route {
  model() {
    return this.store.findAll('user');
  }
}
```

In this case, the "users" route defines a `model()` method that loads all users from the application's store. When a user accesses the "/users" URL, Ember.js automatically executes the `model()` method of the "users" route to retrieve the necessary data to display the list of users.

2. Model:
The Model in Ember.js represents the underlying data of the application. Models are defined within the "app/models" directory and extend from the EmberObject class. Models can be either individual objects or collections of objects and include attributes that represent

the data to be stored and manipulated within the application.

Continuing with the example of an application that manages a list of users, we could have a model to represent a single user with attributes such as first name, last name, email, etc. The definition of this model could look like this:

```javascript
// app/models/user.js
import EmberObject from '@ember/object';

export default EmberObject.extend({
  firstName: null,
  lastName: null,
  email: null,
});
```

In an Ember.js application model, you can define methods and computed properties to manipulate and interact with data in complex ways. For example, we could define a method to calculate the user's full name by combining the first name and last name.

3. Controller:
The Controller in Ember.js handles user interface logic and data present in models.

Controllers are defined within the "app/controllers" directory and extend from the EmberController class. Controllers are used to expose data to templates and to add or modify logic related to data presentation.

In our example of an application that manages a list of users, we could have a controller called "users" that handles displaying the list of users and managing actions related to users themselves. The definition of this controller could look like this:

```javascript
// app/controllers/users.js
import Controller from '@ember/controller';

export default class UsersController extends Controller {
  // Computed property to order users by name
  sortedUsers: Ember.computed('model.@each.firstName', function() {
    return this.get('model').sortBy('firstName');
  }),

  // Method to delete a user
  deleteUser(user) {
    user.destroyRecord();
  }
```

```
}
```

In the "users" controller, we can define computed properties to manipulate the data present in the model and actions to handle user interactions with the interface. For example, we could define a computed property to order users by name and an action to delete a user from the list.

In conclusion, Route, Model, Controller are three key concepts in Ember.js that allow for organizing and managing the application in a modular and scalable way. Route handles application navigation, Model represents underlying data, and Controller manages user interface logic. By effectively integrating these three concepts, it is possible to create complex and dynamic web applications with Ember.js.

Let's say we have a simple application that displays a list of blog posts. In this scenario, we would create a route for the "posts" resource, a model to fetch the data from the server, and a controller to handle any additional logic and pass data to the template.

First, we define the route for the "posts" resource in the routes/ folder:

```javascript
// routes/posts.js

import Route from '@ember/routing/route';

export default class PostsRoute extends Route {
  model() {
    return this.store.findAll('post');
  }
}
```

Next, we create a model to fetch the data from the server in the models/ folder:

```javascript
// models/post.js

import Model, { attr } from '@ember-data/model';

export default class PostModel extends Model {
  @attr('string') title;
  @attr('string') body;
}
```

```

Finally, we implement a controller to handle any additional logic and data manipulation in the controllers/ folder:

```javascript
// controllers/posts.js

import Controller from '@ember/controller';

export default class PostsController extends Controller {
  // Additional logic can go here
}
```

By following the Route Model Controller pattern in Ember.js, we can keep our application organized and easily maintainable. Each component has a clear responsibility, making it easier to debug and extend the application in the future.
```

5. Using Ember CLI to generate a new Ember.js project Basic structure of an Ember.js project

Ember.js is an open-source JavaScript framework that allows you to create complex and scalable web applications. One of its main features is its MVC (Model-View-Controller) structure that helps organize the code of applications in a clear and hierarchical way. In this article, we will see how to create a new Ember.js application using Ember CLI and the basic structure of an Ember.js project.

Ember CLI is a command-line tool that allows you to easily and quickly generate new Ember.js projects. First of all, make sure you have npm (Node Package Manager) installed on your computer, as Ember CLI is installed via npm. Once npm is installed, you can install Ember CLI by running the command:

```
npm install -g ember-cli
```

Once Ember CLI has been successfully installed, you can create a new Ember.js project by running the following command:

```
ember new project_name
```

Where `project_name` is the name you want to give to the project. This command will create a new folder with the project name inside the current directory and generate the basic structure of an Ember.js project.

Once the project is generated, you can navigate to the project folder using the command `cd project_name` and start the Ember.js application using the command:

```
ember serve
```

This command will start a local server and make the Ember.js application available at http://localhost:4200 in the browser.

The basic structure of an Ember.js project is organized hierarchically following the MVC pattern. Here is an overview of the main elements of an Ember.js project:

1. `app/`: This folder contains all the source files of the Ember.js application. Inside this folder, you will find the files `app.js`, `router.js`, and `templates/` which are used to define the application logic and the handlebars templates used to generate the user interface.

2. `public/`: This folder contains static files such as images, stylesheets, and JavaScript files that do not need to be processed by Ember CLI.

3. `tests/`: This folder contains the tests of the Ember.js application. Unit tests and integration tests can be written using Ember.js's built-in testing framework, QUnit.

4. `vendor/`: This folder contains third-party libraries used by the Ember.js application. Here you can include libraries like Bootstrap, jQuery, or other external plugins.

The main files of an Ember.js project are `app.js` and `router.js`. In the `app.js` file, the models, controllers, and components of the application are defined. In the `router.js` file, the routing of the application is defined, i.e. the paths that are associated with certain templates and controllers.

Handlebars templates are used to define the user interface of the Ember.js application. Handlebars templates can include variables, loops, and conditions to dynamically generate HTML code. Handlebars templates are defined inside the `templates/` folder and can be associated with specific controllers using the routing defined in the `router.js` file.

Ember.js is a powerful JavaScript framework for creating complex and scalable web applications. By using Ember CLI, you can quickly generate new Ember.js projects and leverage the MVC structure to organize the application code clearly. With a good understanding of the basic structure of an Ember.js project and its main components, you can start creating advanced web applications using this framework.

To create a new Ember.js project using Ember CLI, you can follow these steps:

1. Install Ember CLI globally by running the command:
```

npm install -g ember-cli
```

2. Create a new Ember project by running the command:
```
ember new my-ember-app
```

3. Navigate into the newly created project directory:
```
cd my-ember-app
```

4. Start the development server by running the command:
```
ember serve
```

5. You can now access your Ember application at `http://localhost:4200` in your browser.

The basic structure of an Ember.js project includes various directories such as `app`, `tests`, and `public` along with various configuration files. The `app` directory contains the main application code including routes, components, and templates. The `tests` directory contains all the test files for the project, while the `public` directory holds static assets like images and fonts. Additionally, Ember CLI provides a powerful set of tools to easily manage dependencies, build the project, and run tests. By following these steps, you can quickly set up a new Ember.js project and start building your application with ease.

6. Dynamic User Interfaces with Ember.js Using Handlebars for Template Creation

One of the key features of Ember.js is its ability to efficiently handle template creation through the use of Handlebars, a lightweight and powerful templating engine that allows for easy creation of dynamic and responsive user interfaces.

Handlebars is a templating system that is based on a markup syntax very similar to HTML, but with the ability to add dynamism through the use of expressions and helpers. Thanks to Handlebars, it is possible to create reusable and maintainable templates, making it easier to manage and display data in the web application developed with Ember.js.

To use Handlebars with Ember.js, it is necessary to define the templates within specific folder and file structures, following the conventions established by the framework. For example, you can define a template for displaying a list of items within a "templates" folder and give a meaningful name to the file, such as "items-list.hbs".

Within the template file, you can use Handlebars syntax for inserting and manipulating data. For example, you can use the Handlebars expression {{#each}} to iterate over a list of items and display them within the template. Additionally, you can define custom variables and helpers to manage data visualization in a more flexible and dynamic way.

Another advantage of using Handlebars with Ember.js is the ability to define reusable components and independent modules that can be easily integrated within the main application template. Thanks to Handlebars, you can define templates for individual components and use them within other templates, facilitating the creation of complex and modular user interfaces.

To use Handlebars with Ember.js, it is important to have a good understanding of how templates work and how they interact with the rest of the application. Here is an example of how to use Handlebars to create a simple template with Ember.js:

```handlebars
{{! This is a Handlebars comment }}
```

```html
<div class="user-profile">
  <h2>{{title}}</h2>
  <p>{{description}}</p>
</div>
```

In this example, the Handlebars template defines an HTML block with two variables `title` and `description`. These variables can be dynamically replaced with data coming from the Ember.js application.

To associate the template with the application data, you can use the Ember.js controller. Here is an example of a controller that provides data to the template:

```javascript
import Controller from '@ember/controller';

export default Controller.extend({
  title: 'Welcome!',
  description: 'This is an example of a Handlebars template with Ember.js'
});
```

With this controller, the `title` and `description` data are passed to the Handlebars template and displayed dynamically in the user interface. This is just a simple example of how to use Handlebars with Ember.js to create dynamic and responsive user interfaces. With some practice, you can fully leverage the potential of these tools to create modern and engaging web applications.

7. Event Management in the User Interface in Ember.js

Ember.js is an open-source web development framework based on the Model View Controller (MVC) architectural pattern that offers excellent event management in the user interface. Events are responsible for interacting with the user and handling the actions they perform within the web application. In this context, Ember.js offers various features to efficiently and intuitively handle events.

In Ember.js, events within the user interface are primarily managed through Actions. Actions are functions defined within controllers and components that are triggered by events such as button clicks, form submissions, or mouse hover over an element. Actions are very versatile and can be passed from a controller to a component, allowing for centralized event management within the application.

To define an Action within a controller, you can use the `actions` method, which declares the various actions you want to handle. For example:

```javascript
import Controller from '@ember/controller';

export default Controller.extend({
  actions: {
    submitForm() {
      // Handle form submission
    },
    toggleMenu() {
      // Handle menu click
    }
  }
});
```

Once an Action is defined within a controller, you can link it to an HTML element in the user interface using the `{{action}}` modifier. For example:

```handlebars
<button {{action "submitForm"}}>Submit</button>
```

This way, when the user clicks the "Submit" button, the `submitForm` Action defined in the controller is triggered. This mechanism allows for separating event handling logic from the user interface presentation, following the principle of separation of concerns.

Additionally, Ember.js allows passing parameters to Actions, allowing for customizing behavior based on specific event information. For example:

```handlebars
<button {{action "deleteItem" item}}>Delete</button>
```

In this case, the `deleteItem` Action receives the `item` object as a parameter, allowing for identifying the item to delete.

In addition to Actions, Ember.js also provides an event system based on the Observer Pattern, allowing for observing and reacting to state changes within the application. Observers are useful for monitoring data changes and updating the user interface accordingly. For example:

```javascript
import Component from '@ember/component';
```

```javascript
export default Component.extend({
  status: 'Online',

  statusObserver: Ember.observer('status', function() {
    // Code to execute when status changes
  })
});
```

In this case, the `statusObserver` observes the change in the `status` state within the component and triggers a callback function every time the state is modified. This mechanism allows for automatically keeping the user interface synchronized with the application state.

Furthermore, Ember.js also offers the ability to handle global events through the `Ember.Evented` service. This service allows for creating and handling custom events within the application, enabling efficient communication between different components and controllers. For example:

```javascript
import Service from '@ember/service';
import Ember from 'ember';
```

```
export default Service.extend(Ember.Evented, {
  init() {
    this._super(...arguments);

    this.on('userAuthenticated', function() {
      // Code to execute when the user authenticates
    });
  }
});
```

In this case, the `Ember.Evented` service provides the ability to create a custom event `userAuthenticated` that is triggered when the user authenticates within the application. This mechanism enables efficient communication between different components and controllers, allowing for a more consistent and centralized event handling.

In conclusion, Ember.js offers a powerful and intuitive event handling within the user interface, allowing for efficient and structured management of user actions. Through Actions, observers, and the `Ember.Evented` service, it is possible to create a responsive and dynamic user interface that follows the principles of the

MVC pattern and provides an optimal user experience.

8. Testing in Ember.js Types of tests supported in Ember.js
Using QUnit to write tests

Ember.js is an open-source web development framework that facilitates the creation of complex and scalable web applications using the JavaScript language. One crucial aspect in the development of any application is testing, which allows verifying that the code is correct and that the functionalities respond correctly to the specifications.

Ember.js supports different types of tests to ensure code quality and ensure that the application functions correctly. The main types of tests supported in Ember.js are:

1. Unit Testing: This type of test focuses on isolating individual units of code, such as functions or methods. The goal is to verify that each unit functions correctly independently of the others. Unit tests are written to check that the produced code works as expected.

2. Integration Testing: Integration tests verify how different units of code interact with each

other. These tests focus on the interactions between the various components of the application and ensure that the units work together correctly. Integration tests are essential to ensure that the application has a cohesive logic and functions correctly as a whole.

3. Acceptance Testing: This type of test verifies the behavior of the application from a real-world usage perspective, simulating the actions that a user might take. Acceptance tests are useful to check the application's functionalities from start to finish and ensure that they correctly respond to user needs.

Each type of test has its role in the Ember.js testing ecosystem and contributes to ensuring code stability and quality. One of the most commonly used tools for writing tests in Ember.js is QUnit, a JavaScript testing framework developed by jQuery to facilitate test writing and automated test execution.

QUnit provides a simple and intuitive syntax for creating tests and verifying that the code functions correctly. Tests written with QUnit can be executed in different environments, such as the browser or Node.js, and provide a clear overview of the code status and potential issues.

To use QUnit to write tests in Ember.js, it is necessary to install the ember-qunit package via npm. This package provides a set of utilities and tools for writing tests in Ember.js using QUnit syntax.

An example of how to use QUnit to write tests in Ember.js is as follows:

In this example, a test module is defined for an Ember.js controller using QUnit syntax. Within the module, two tests are defined: one to check that the controller exists and a second test to verify that the controller correctly calculates a value based on an input.

QUnit offers a range of methods and assertions to verify that the code works correctly and produce clear and concise results. By using QUnit to write tests in Ember.js, you can ensure the quality and stability of the code and ensure that the application functions correctly in every situation.

Tests are a fundamental aspect in the development of any application and play a key role in ensuring that the code is correct and that the features meet the specifications. Using QUnit to write tests in Ember.js provides a simple and effective way to verify the quality of the code and ensure that the application works correctly.

9. Deploying an Ember.js Application: Preparing the Application for Deployment

Deploying an Ember.js application is an important process that ensures the application is ready to be distributed and used by end users. Before proceeding with deployment, it is necessary to prepare the application by following a series of steps to ensure everything is configured correctly and the application is optimized for performance.

The first step in preparing an Ember.js application for deployment is to ensure that all necessary dependencies and modules are installed correctly. Using npm (Node Package Manager), you can install all the dependency packages listed in the package.json file. It is important to ensure that all dependencies are updated to the latest version to ensure compatibility and stability of the application.

Once all dependencies are installed, the application needs to be built to generate the necessary files for deployment. This process can be done using the `ember build` command from the terminal. This command will compile the application and create a `dist` directory containing all the files needed for deployment.

Before proceeding with deployment, it is important to configure the hosting environment where the application will be hosted. If using a hosting service like Heroku, you will need to create an account and correctly configure the application to be hosted on this service. This may include configuring environment variables, configuration files, and specific parameters of the hosting service.

Once the hosting environment is configured, you can proceed with deploying the application. There are several ways to deploy an Ember.js application, including using hosting services like Heroku, Firebase, or Netlify, or deploying to a traditional web server like Apache or Nginx.

To deploy the application on Heroku, you can use the `git subtree push --prefix dist heroku master` command from the terminal to upload the `dist` directory to Heroku and deploy the application. This process will ensure the application is accessible online and ready to be used by end users.

After deploying the application, it is important to monitor performance and availability to ensure everything is functioning correctly. By using monitoring tools like New Relic or Sentry, you can track any issues or errors that may arise and address them promptly to ensure an optimal user experience.

Ember.js is an open-source framework for developing web applications in JavaScript, known for its organized structure and ease of use. Before deploying an Ember.js application, it is important to properly prepare the application to ensure it functions correctly once it is published.

Here is a detailed guide on how to prepare an Ember.js application for deployment:

1. Make sure you have Node.js and npm installed on your computer. Node.js is a JavaScript runtime environment that allows you to run JavaScript code outside of a browser, while npm is a package manager for Node.js that makes it easy to install dependencies and modules.

2. Create a `.gitignore` file in the project root and add the following files and folders to it:

```
/dist/
/tmp/
/node_modules/
/bower_components/
/vendor/
*.log
```

This file is used to exclude unnecessary files and folders from the Git repository and the deployment package.

3. Configure the application correctly for the production environment. This means setting up environment variables properly, using third-party services correctly, and configuring static resources like images, JavaScript files, and CSS files.

4. Update project dependencies by running the `npm update` command. This will ensure that all project dependencies are updated to the latest version and work correctly once published.

5. Optimize the application to improve performance and reduce loading times. This includes minimizing and concatenating JavaScript files, compressing images, and using CDNs for static resources.

6. Run tests to verify that the application functions correctly and that there are no errors or bugs before deployment. You can use tools like QUnit or Mocha to run unit and integration tests.

7. Configure the deployment server. You can use services like Heroku, Firebase, or Netlify to deploy an Ember.js application quickly and easily. Make sure to follow the specific instructions for the chosen deployment service and properly configure the server configuration file.

8. Run the `ember build --environment=production` command to generate the optimized version of the application ready for deployment. This command creates a `dist/` folder in the project root that contains all the files needed for deployment.

9. Deploy the application using the chosen service. This can be done through a graphical interface or via the command line, depending on the preferences and ease of use of the chosen service.

10. Verify that the application is running

correctly on the deployment server and that all features are active and functioning. Conduct regression tests to ensure there are no errors or bugs in the new production environment.

Here is an example of how to prepare an Ember.js application for deployment using Heroku as the deployment service:

1. Make sure you have a Heroku account and have installed Heroku CLI on your computer.

2. Create a new Ember.js project using the `ember new project-name` command.

3. Update the project dependencies by running the `npm update` command.

4. Creare un file `.gitignore` nella root del progetto e aggiungere i file e le cartelle non necessari al repository Git.

5. Configurare l'applicazione per l'ambiente di produzione utilizzando le variabili d'ambiente e i servizi di terze parti.

6. Eseguire i test per verificare che l'applicazione funzioni correttamente.

7. Eseguire il comando `ember build

`--environment=production` per generare la versione ottimizzata dell'applicazione.

8. Creare un file `Procfile` nella root del progetto con il seguente contenuto:

```
web: node server.js
```

Questo file indica a Heroku come eseguire l'applicazione una volta deployata.

9. Creare un file `server.js` nella root del progetto con il seguente contenuto:

```
const express = require('express');
const path = require('path');
const app = express();

app.use(express.static(path.join(__dirname, 'dist')));

app.get('*', function(req, res) {
  res.sendFile(path.join(__dirname, 'dist/index.html'));
});

const PORT = process.env.PORT || 3000;
app.listen(PORT, () => {
```

```
  console.log(`Server is running on port ${PORT}`);
});
```

Questo file definisce un server Express che serve i file statici presenti nella cartella `dist/` generata dal comando `ember build --environment=production`.

10. Creare un nuovo repository Git e fare il commit dei file del progetto.

11. Collegare il repository Git a Heroku utilizzando il comando `heroku git:remote -a nome-app-heroku`.

12. Effettuare il deploy dell'applicazione sul server Heroku utilizzando il comando `git push heroku master`.

Una volta completati questi passaggi, l'applicazione Ember.js sarà live su Heroku e sarà possibile accedervi tramite il link generato dal servizio. Assicurarsi di monitorare l'applicazione per eventuali errori o problemi e di effettuare aggiornamenti regolari per migliorare le prestazioni e la sicurezza dell'applicazione.

Il deploy di un'applicazione Ember.js è un processo importante che richiede attenzione ai dettagli e una corretta preparazione dell'applicazione prima della distribuzione. Seguendo i passaggi corretti e utilizzando strumenti adeguati è possibile garantire che l'applicazione sia pronta per essere utilizzata online e che funzioni correttamente per gli utenti finali.

10. Performance Optimization Best Practices for Improving performance Tools for Profiling and Optimizing Ember.js

Ember.js is a widely used open-source JavaScript framework for developing large and complex web applications. Like any framework, Ember.js can face performance issues if not used correctly. Optimizing the performance of an Ember.js application is an important process to ensure that the application responds efficiently to user requests and provides a high-quality user experience.

There are several best practices for optimizing the performance of an Ember.js application. In this article, we will examine some of these best practices and also look at some useful tools for profiling and optimizing Ember.js.

Best practices for improving Ember.js performance:

1. Use Ember Data efficiently: Ember Data is a data management library in an Ember.js application. To achieve optimal performance, it is important to use Ember Data efficiently.

For example, you can reduce the number of network calls made by the application by using the findAll method to retrieve all necessary data in a single network call instead of making multiple separate calls to retrieve different data. Additionally, you can use prefetching to proactively retrieve data that may be needed in the future.

2. Optimize view rendering: View rendering is a fundamental part of Ember.js application performance. It is important to avoid excessive view rendering and minimize performance impact. For example, you can use Ember's differential rendering mechanism to render only parts of views that have been changed instead of rendering the entire view every time a change occurs.

3. Use Ember Run Loop appropriately: Ember Run Loop is the mechanism through which Ember.js manages events and actions in the application. It is important to use Ember Run Loop appropriately to ensure that actions are executed efficiently and synchronized. For example, you can use Ember.run.later to delay the execution of an action to avoid browser overload.

4. Optimize state management in the

application: State management is a critical aspect of Ember.js application performance. It is important to organize and manage the application state efficiently to ensure that the application responds quickly and smoothly. For example, you can use Ember Service to manage shared state between different parts of the application and avoid duplicating information in the application state.

5. Use Ember CLI for project management: Ember CLI is a powerful tool for managing and developing Ember.js projects. By using Ember CLI, you can optimize the project structure and automate many common tasks during application development. For example, Ember CLI provides tools for automatic code generation, dependency management, and optimized code compilation for deployment.

Tools for profiling and optimizing Ember.js:

1. Ember Inspector: Ember Inspector is a browser extension that provides debugging and profiling tools for Ember.js applications. With Ember Inspector, you can examine the application state, track actions, view rendering time, and more. Ember Inspector is an essential tool for optimizing the performance of an Ember.js application.

2. Ember Perf: Ember Perf is a performance profiling tool for Ember.js applications. With Ember Perf, you can measure application performance, identify performance issues, and pinpoint areas that require optimization. Ember Perf provides detailed information on view rendering time, network calls, and other critical performance metrics for improving application performance.

3. Chrome DevTools: Chrome DevTools is a development tool integrated into the Chrome browser that provides advanced tools for profiling the performance of web applications. With Chrome DevTools, you can track CPU usage, network calls, memory usage, and other profiling tasks to identify performance issues and optimize the Ember.js application.

Optimizing the performance of an Ember.js application is an important process to ensure that the application responds efficiently and provides a high-quality user experience. By using best practices and appropriate tools for profiling and optimizing Ember.js, you can significantly improve the performance of the application and provide users with a fast and responsive web application.

Performance optimization is a critical aspect of web development, especially when working with complex frameworks like Ember.js. Optimizing the performance of your Ember.js applications can significantly improve the user experience and lead to better conversion rates. In this article, we will discuss some best practices for improving performance and introduce tools for profiling and optimizing Ember.js.

One of the key best practices for improving the performance of Ember.js applications is to reduce the number of DOM manipulations. Ember.js is a data-driven framework, which means that any changes to the data will trigger updates to the DOM. However, excessive DOM manipulations can slow down your application and make it less responsive. To optimize performance, you should try to minimize the number of DOM manipulations by using Ember's computed properties and bindings efficiently.

Another best practice for improving performance is to avoid unnecessary re-renders. Ember.js uses a concept called "re-rendering" to update the DOM when the data changes. However, re-rendering can be costly in terms of performance, especially if you have a large number of components in your application. To avoid unnecessary re-renders, you should use Ember's computed properties and lifecycle hooks to control when components should re-render.

Additionally, you should pay attention to the size of your Ember.js application bundle. Large bundles can slow down your application's performance, especially on mobile devices with limited resources. To optimize the size of your bundle, you should use tools like webpack and ember-cli-deploy to bundle and minify your code efficiently. You can also use code splitting techniques to load only the necessary code on demand, reducing the initial load time of your application.

In addition to these best practices, there are several tools available for profiling and optimizing Ember.js applications. One of the most popular tools is the Ember Inspector, which is a browser extension that allows you to inspect and debug your Ember.js application in real-time. With the Ember Inspector, you can view the state of your application, track changes to the data, and debug performance issues.

Another useful tool for profiling Ember.js applications is the Chrome DevTools Performance panel. This tool allows you to record and analyze the performance of your application, including CPU usage, memory usage, and network requests. By using the Performance panel, you can identify performance bottlenecks and optimize your code accordingly.

Furthermore, you can use tools like Ember CLI Mirage to simulate server responses and test your application's performance under different network conditions. By simulating various scenarios, you can identify potential performance issues and optimize your code before deploying it to production.

In conclusion, optimizing the performance of your Ember.js applications is essential for delivering a fast and responsive user experience. By following best practices such as reducing DOM manipulations, avoiding unnecessary re-renders, and optimizing the size of your bundle, you can improve the performance of your Ember.js applications significantly. Additionally, by using tools for profiling and optimizing Ember.js, you can identify performance bottlenecks and optimize your code efficiently.

11. Glossary Terms and Key Concepts of Ember.js

Ember.js is an open-source framework for building client-side web applications based on JavaScript. It is designed to simplify the development process of complex web applications, providing an organized and well-defined structure for managing data, user interface, and business logic. In this glossary, we will look at the main terms and key concepts of Ember.js.

1. **Framework**: Ember.js is a JavaScript framework, which is a pre-defined code library that provides a structure and conventions for web application development. Ember.js includes a set of pre-defined components and features to streamline the development process and improve code maintainability.

2. **Convention over Configuration**: Ember.js follows the principle of "convention over configuration," which means that many design decisions are automatically made based on default conventions rather than requiring explicit configurations from the developer.

This approach helps to reduce code complexity and speed up application development.

3. **Dependency Injection**: Ember.js automatically manages dependency resolution between different components of the application. When one component depends on another component, Ember.js takes care of loading and initializing the necessary resources, ensuring that everything functions correctly.

4. **Components**: In Ember.js, components are reusable and self-contained UI elements. Each component has its own logic and associated template and can be easily inserted into different parts of the application. Components promote modular design and increased code reusability.

5. **Route**: Routes in Ember.js handle application routing, which involves navigating between different pages and states of the application. Each route defines a data model to display and an associated template. Routes can capture parameters from the URL and retrieve the necessary data to display the corresponding page.

6. **Controller**: Controllers in Ember.js act as an intermediary between data models and application views. They manage presentation logic and event handling, allowing the separation of business logic from visual presentation.

7. **Data Model (Model)**: The data model in Ember.js represents the state of the application and defines the structure and constraints of the data used by the application. Models can be retrieved from a remote server via API calls or generated locally within the application.

8. **Template**: The template in Ember.js defines the HTML structure and layout of the web page. Templates can include JavaScript code for dynamic data processing and can also include Ember.js-specific components, directives, and helpers to extend the standard HTML functionalities.

9. **Application Instance (Application)**: The application instance in Ember.js represents the main instance of the application and contains all the components, controllers, and routes used by the application. The application instance is responsible for managing the global state of the application

and coordinating the different parts of the application.

10. **Binding (Binding)**: Bindings in Ember.js are mechanisms for automatically synchronizing data between different components of the application. When data changes in one component, the binding automatically propagates the change to other interested components, ensuring that data is always up-to-date and synchronized.

11. **Computed Property**: Computed properties in Ember.js are dynamically calculated properties based on one or more input values. Computed properties allow for defining complex data calculation logic without having to manually update values every time one of the inputs changes.

12. **Handlebars**: Handlebars is a templating engine used by Ember.js for creating dynamic templates. Handlebars allows for inserting JavaScript expressions within HTML code for dynamic content generation. Ember.js extends Handlebars by introducing new directives and framework-specific functionalities.

13. **Router (Router)**: The router in Ember.js manages application navigation

between different routes and controls the loading and displaying of associated templates. The router defines the application's routing rules and manages transitions between pages.

These are just some of the main terms and key concepts of Ember.js. The framework offers many advanced features and design conventions that can help developers create sophisticated and robust web applications. With a good understanding of these concepts, it is possible to leverage the full potential of Ember.js and create modern and high-performing web applications.

12. Ember.js Syntax

Ember.js is an open-source front-end development framework based on JavaScript that follows the Model-View-ViewModel (MVVM) architectural pattern.

Ember.js simplifies the development of complex web applications by providing a structured and consistent framework for building dynamic and interactive user interfaces. Its main goal is to simplify the management of application state and communication between components, allowing developers to focus on business logic and user experience.

The syntax of Ember.js is designed to be clear, intuitive, and easy to learn. In the following example, we will explore some of the fundamental concepts of Ember.js syntax:

1. Routing: Ember.js uses a routing system to handle navigation between different pages of the application. Routing in Ember.js is managed through the `router.js` file, which defines the various routes of our application.

Example of defining a route in `router.js`:

```javascript
Router.map(function() {
  this.route('home');
  this.route('about');
  this.route('contact');
});
```

2. Model: In Ember.js, models represent the application data and are used to interact with the backend or API service. Models are defined using Ember Data, a data management library integrated into Ember.js.

Example of defining a model in Ember.js:

```javascript
import DS from 'ember-data';

const { Model } = DS;

export default Model.extend({
  title: DS.attr('string'),
  description: DS.attr('string'),
  ...
});
```

3. Controller: Controllers are used to manage business logic and coordinate user actions within the application. Controllers in Ember.js are responsible for manipulating data and updating models based on user interactions.

Example of defining a controller in Ember.js:

```javascript
import Controller from '@ember/controller';

export default Controller.extend({
  actions: {
    updateModel(data) {
      this.model.setProperties(data);
      this.model.save();
    },
    ...
  }
});
```

4. Component: Components are reusable code blocks that represent parts of the application's user interface. Components in Ember.js are used to separate user interface logic from business logic and create custom components that can be easily integrated into the application.

Example of defining a component in Ember.js:

```javascript
import Component from '@ember/component';

export default Component.extend({
  classNames: ['my-component'],
  ...
});
```

5. Template: Templates are markup files used to define the application's user interface. Templates in Ember.js are written using Handlebars, a templating language that allows dynamically embedding data and logic within the markup.

Example of defining a template in Ember.js:

```handlebars
{{#each model as |item|}}
  <div>{{item.title}}</div>
{{/each}}
```

6. Service: Services are used to share business logic and data between different components of the application. Services in Ember.js are singleton objects that can be injected into controllers, components, and routes for shared access to application data and logic.

Example of defining a service in Ember.js:

```javascript
import Service from '@ember/service';

export default Service.extend({
  data: [],
  ...
});
```

7. Promises and async/await: Ember.js supports the use of promises and async/await for handling asynchronous operations within the application. Promises efficiently manage API calls and asynchronous I/O operations, while async/await simplifies control flow

management within asynchronous code.

Example of using async/await in Ember.js:

```javascript
import Route from '@ember/routing/route';

export default Route.extend({
  async model() {
    return await this.store.findAll('post');
  }
});
```

The syntax of Ember.js provides a variety of tools and techniques to ease the development of complex web applications. This example provides an introduction to the fundamental concepts of Ember.js syntax and shows how these concepts can be used to build responsive and scalable web applications.

Ember.js is a powerful and flexible framework that gives developers a solid foundation for building modern web applications. With its clear and intuitive syntax, Ember.js is a popular choice for developing projects of various complexities and sizes.

13. Ember.js Benefits

Ember.js is an open-source framework that allows for the effective and efficient development of complex web applications. Based on the Model-View-Controller (MVC) architectural pattern, Ember.js offers a range of advantages that make it a popular choice among web developers.

One of the key benefits of using Ember.js is its powerful application state management capabilities. With a state management system based on URLs, Ember.js enables developers to easily create dynamic and responsive web applications. This means that users can update the page and navigate between different sections of the application without having to reload the entire page each time.

Another advantage of Ember.js is its preference for conventions over configurations. This allows developers to save time and effort by avoiding the need to make decisions on how to structure the application. Ember.js provides a set of default conventions that simplify code writing and promote consistent and organized development.

Furthermore, Ember.js offers a wide range of tools and libraries to simplify the development of complex web applications. One of the most popular features of Ember.js is its rich library of reusable components. Ember.js components allow developers to create custom and modular user interface elements that can easily be integrated into different parts of the application.

Another benefit of Ember.js is its tight integration with Ember Data, a data management library that greatly simplifies data reading and writing operations to and from the backend. Ember Data handles communication with the server, data caching, and synchronization via WebSocket, allowing developers to focus on application logic without manually managing data operations.

Ember.js also provides a flexible and powerful routing system that enables developers to easily manage different application pages and handle URL parameters in a simple and intuitive way. Additionally, Ember.js supports the concept of nested routes, allowing for the creation of nested route hierarchies for more efficient navigation within the application.

Another advantage of using Ember.js is its active developer community and the availability of extensive online documentation and resources. The Ember.js community is highly active and regularly organizes events, conferences, and hackathons to promote knowledge sharing and continuously improve the framework. Additionally, Ember.js has comprehensive and well-structured documentation covering all aspects of the framework, from basics to solving complex issues.

Finally, Ember.js is well-supported by a range of tools and plugins that streamline development and enhance developer productivity. For example, Ember CLI is a command-line tool that simplifies the creation, compilation, and testing of Ember.js applications. Additionally, Ember Inspector is a browser plugin that provides an advanced debugging tool to analyze and modify application behavior in real-time.

Ember.js is a powerful and flexible framework that offers numerous benefits for the development of complex web applications. With its advanced state management, default conventions, reusable component libraries, and tight integration with Ember Data,

Ember.js allows developers to easily create robust, responsive, and scalable web applications. Its active community and availability of extensive online documentation and resources make it a popular choice among web developers seeking a comprehensive and well-supported solution for creating modern web applications.

14. Examples of Ember.js code

Ember.js is an open-source JavaScript framework that facilitates the development of complex web applications through the implementation of the Model-View-Controller (MVC) architectural pattern. In this guide, we will explore several examples of Ember.js code to understand how we can use this framework to create dynamic and interactive web applications.

1. Creating an Ember.js application
To start using Ember.js, you first need to create a basic application. Here is an example of code to create a simple Ember.js application:

```
// Define our Ember application
var App = Ember.Application.create();

// Define a basic route for our application
App.Router.map(function() {
  // Insert application routes here
});

// Define a basic controller for our application
```

```
App.IndexController = Ember.Controller.extend({
  // Define controller properties and methods here
});

// Define a basic view for our application
App.IndexView = Ember.View.extend({
  // Define view properties and methods here
});
```

In this example, we are defining a simple Ember.js application with a basic route, controller, and view. These will be the main components of our application that will allow us to manage presentation logic and user interaction.

2. Defining a model
One fundamental aspect of Ember.js is data management through models. Here is an example of code to define a model in Ember.js:

```
// Define a basic model for our data
App.Post = Ember.Object.extend({
  title: null,
  content: null
```

```
});
```

In this example, we are defining a basic model called "Post" with two attributes: "title" and "content". This model will be used to represent data related to posts within our application.

3. Retrieving data from an API
To retrieve data from an external API and display it within our Ember.js application, we can use the Ember Data service. Here is an example of code to retrieve data from an API and display it in a route:

```
// Define a model for posts
App.Post = DS.Model.extend({
  title: DS.attr('string'),
  content: DS.attr('string')
});

// Define a route to display posts
App.PostsRoute = Ember.Route.extend({
  model() {
    return this.store.findAll('post');
  }
});
```

In this example, we are defining a "Post" model using Ember Data and a "PostsRoute" route to retrieve all the posts from our API and display them within our application. This allows us to efficiently manage data within our Ember.js application.

4. Creating a component
Components are an essential part of Ember.js that allow us to create reusable elements within our application. Here is an example of code to create an Ember.js component:

```
// Define a component to display a single post
App.PostComponent = Ember.Component.extend({
  tagName: 'div',
  classNames: ['post'],
  post: null
});
```

In this example, we are defining a "PostComponent" component that will display a single post within our application. This component can be easily reused at different points in the application to display posts consistently.

5. Event handling

Ember.js offers an event handling system that allows us to interact with elements in our application and manage user actions. Here is an example of code to handle a click event on a button within an Ember.js template:

```
// Define a controller for our application
App.ButtonController = Ember.Controller.extend({
  actions: {
    handleClick() {
      // Add logic here to handle the button click
      console.log('Button clicked!');
    }
  }
});
```

In this example, we are defining a "ButtonController" controller with a "handleClick" action that will be executed when the user clicks on a button within the template. This allows us to easily manage user events and actions within our Ember.js application.

In conclusion, these are just a few examples of

Ember.js code that demonstrate how we can use this framework to create dynamic and interactive web applications. With Ember.js, we can efficiently manage data, create complex user interfaces, and handle user events in a practical and intuitive manner. I hope this guide has been helpful in understanding the features and capabilities of Ember.js in the realm of web application development.

Ember.js is an open-source web development framework based on JavaScript that helps developers create complex and scalable web applications. Its design following the MVC (Model-View-Controller) pattern makes it ideal for creating interactive and dynamic web applications. Below are code examples that illustrate how to use Ember.js to create components and services.

Example 1: Creating a component

```javascript
// Definition of a component named 'hello-world'
import Component from '@ember/component';

export default Component.extend({
  message: "Hello, world!"
});
```

```handlebars
<!-- Using the 'hello-world' component in a page template -->
<h1>{{hello-world}}</h1>
```

In this example, we created a component named 'hello-world' that displays a greeting message. In the page template, we use the 'hello-world' component to display the message.

Example 2: Creating a service

```javascript
// Definition of a service named 'user-status'
import Service from '@ember/service';

export default Service.extend({
  currentUser: null,

  setCurrentUser(user) {
    this.set("currentUser", user);
  },

  getCurrentUser() {
    return this.get("currentUser");
  }
});
```

```javascript
// Using the 'user-status' service in a controller
import Controller from '@ember/controller';
import { inject as service } from '@ember/service';
```

```javascript
export default Controller.extend({
  userStatus: service(),

  init() {
    this._super(...arguments);

    // Setting the current user using the 'user-status' service
    this.userStatus.setCurrentUser("Alice");
  }
});
```

In this example, we created a service named 'user-status' that manages the current user's status. In the controller, we use the 'user-status' service to set and get the current user.

Example 3: Creating a model and model relationships

```javascript
// Definition of two models, 'post' and 'comment', with a one-to-many relationship
import Model from '@ember-data/model';
import { hasMany } from 'ember-data/relationships';

export default Model.extend({
```

```
  title: DS.attr('string'),
  body: DS.attr('string'),

  comments: hasMany('comment')
});

import Model from '@ember-data/model';
import { belongsTo } from 'ember-data/relationships';

export default Model.extend({
  text: DS.attr('string'),

  post: belongsTo('post')
});
```

In this example, we defined two models, 'post' and 'comment', with a one-to-many relationship between them. The 'post' model has many comments associated with it, while each comment belongs to a single post.

These are just some code examples illustrating how to use Ember.js to create components, services, and models. With Ember.js, you can quickly and organizedly develop complex and interactive web applications.

Other examples:

Example 1: Creating an Ember component

An Ember component is a way to create reusable elements within your application. Here is an example of creating an Ember component called "hello-world":

```javascript
// components/hello-world.js
import Component from '@glimmer/component';

export default class HelloWorldComponent extends Component {
  greeting = 'Hello, World!';
}
```

The code above defines an Ember component called "hello-world" that displays the message "Hello, World!".

Example 2: Creating an Ember route

An Ember route defines the behavior of the application when a specific URL is visited. Here is an example of creating an Ember route for the URL "/hello":

```javascript
// routes/hello.js
import Route from '@ember/routing/route';

export default class HelloRoute extends Route {
  model() {
    return { name: 'World' };
  }
}
```

The code above defines an Ember route called "hello" that returns an object with the key "name" set to "World" in the `model()` method.

Example 3: Creating an Ember controller

An Ember controller is an object that handles the display logic between the model and the template. Here is an example of creating an Ember controller called "hello":

```javascript
// controllers/hello.js
import Controller from '@ember/controller';
```

```
export default class HelloController extends Controller {
  get greeting() {
    return `Hello, ${this.model.name}!`;
  }
}
```

The code above defines an Ember controller called "hello" that defines a getter `greeting` that returns the greeting message "Hello, {{model name}}!".

Example 4: Using an Ember component in a template

Once you have created an Ember component, you can use it in a Handlebars template. Here is an example of using the "hello-world" component in an Ember template:

```handlebars
<!-- templates/hello.hbs -->
<h1>{{hello-world}}</h1>
```

The code above uses the Ember component "hello-world" in the "hello.hbs" template to display the message "Hello, World!".

With Ember.js, you can easily create reusable components, define your application behavior through routes, and handle display logic with controllers. We hope these examples help you better understand how to use Ember.js in your next project.

Here are some examples of Ember.js code that illustrate its main features and advantages.

1. Creating a new Ember.js project
To start working with Ember.js, you need to create a new project using the Ember CLI command. Here is an example of code to create a new Ember.js project:

```
$ ember new my-new-app
```

This command will create a new directory with the basic structure of an Ember.js project, including main files like app.js, router.js, and template.hbs.

2. Creating a model
One of the fundamental concepts in Ember.js is the model, which represents the application data and is used to interact with the backend. Here is an example of code to create a post model:

```javascript
// models/post.js
import Model from '@ember-data/model';
```

```
export default class PostModel extends Model {
  @attr('string') title;
  @attr('string') body;
  @attr('date') createdAt;
}
```

In this example, the `Post` model contains three attributes: `title`, `body`, and `createdAt`, which are defined using the `@attr` annotation to specify the data type.

3. Creating a controller

A controller in Ember.js is responsible for handling the presentation logic and interaction of the view. Here is an example of code to create a controller to manage the list of posts:

```javascript
// controllers/posts.js
import Controller from '@ember/controller';

export default class PostsController extends Controller {
  queryParams = ['search'];
  search = '';
}
```

In this example, the `PostsController` controller contains a `search` attribute that is used to filter the list of posts based on the text entered by the user.

4. Creating a template
Templates in Ember.js are Handlebars files that define the structure and layout of the view. Here is an example of code to create a template to display the list of posts:

```handlebars
{{!-- templates/posts.hbs --}}
<h1>Post List</h1>

{{input type="text" value=search placeholder="Search posts..."}}

<ul>
  {{#each model as |post|}}
    <li>{{post.title}} - {{post.body}}</li>
  {{/each}}
</ul>
```

In this template, the `each` helper is used to iterate over the list of posts and display the title and body of each post.

5. Creating a route

Routes in Ember.js are responsible for fetching the data needed for the view and preparing it for display. Here is an example of code to create a route to retrieve the list of posts:

```javascript
// routes/posts.js
import Route from '@ember/routing/route';

export default class PostsRoute extends Route {
  model() {
    return this.store.findAll('post');
  }
}
```

In this example, the `PostsRoute` route uses the `model` method to retrieve all records of type `post` from the data store.

6. Creating a component

Components in Ember.js are reusable code blocks that represent a specific part of the user interface. Here is an example of code to create a component to display a single post:

```javascript
// components/post-item.js
```

```
import Component from '@glimmer/component';

export default class PostItemComponent extends Component {
  get formattedDate() {
    return this.args.post.createdAt.toLocaleDateString();
  }
}
```

In this component, a `formattedDate` method is defined that returns the post creation date in the format `dd/mm/yyyy`.

These are just some examples of Ember.js code that illustrate the main features and advantages of the framework. With Ember.js, you can create complex and high-performance web applications in an organized and efficient manner, making the most of the MVC pattern and the many features provided by the framework.

Index

1. Introduction to Ember.js pg.4

2. Fundamentals MVC (Model-View-Controller) Router Template Components Ember.js Services pg.11

3. Ember.js Template Components pg.19

4. Route Model Controller in Ember.js pg.31

5. Using Ember CLI to generate a new Ember.js project Basic structure of an Ember.js project pg.38

6. Dynamic User Interfaces with Ember.js Using Handlebars for Template Creation pg.44

7. Event Management in the User Interface in Ember.js pg.48

8. Testing in Ember.js Types of tests supported in Ember.js Using QUnit to write tests pg.54

9. Deploying an Ember.js Application: Preparing the Application for Deployment pg.58

10. Performance Optimization Best Practices for Improving performance Tools for Profiling and Optimizing Ember.js pg.67

11. Glossary Terms and Key Concepts of Ember.js pg.74

12. Ember.js Syntax pg.79

13. Ember.js Benefits pg.85

14. Examples of Ember.js code pg.89

www.ingramcontent.com/pod-product-compliance
Lightning Source LLC
Chambersburg PA
CBHW050318230526
45471CB00005B/2249